12/10/19

Nazi Germany's Surrender to the Allies
Ending World War II in Europe

UNCONDITIONAL SURRENDER
WITNESSING HISTORY – MAY 1945

PAUL E. ZIGO

ARCHWAY
PUBLISHING

Archway Publishing books may be ordered through booksellers or by contacting:

Archway Publishing
1663 Liberty Drive
Bloomington, IN 47403
www.archwaypublishing.com
1 (888) 242-5904

ISBN: 978-1-4808-8100-6 (sc)
ISBN: 978-1-4808-8101-3 (e)

Library of Congress Control Number: 2019911459

Print information available on the last page.

Archway Publishing rev. date: 08/08/2019

BOOK CREDITS

Paul E. Zigo, author
Director of the World War II Era Studies Institute
Author/editor of *Witnessing History: The Eisenhower Photographs*
Author of *The Longest Walk: The Story of the 29th Infantry Division in Normandy, France, June 6 – July 18, 1944*
Co-Author of *When Men Have to Die – A Memoir of the Bataan Death March*

Credits:
Merry Brennan, text editor
Author, lecturer, professional journalist

Photo credits: World War II photos used throughout the publication courtesy of the U.S. Army Center of Military History, Washington, D.C. and the National Archives, Washington, D.C.

Supportive material provided by former U.S. Army veteran Al Meserlin, General Dwight D. Eisenhower's wartime photographer, September 1944 to July 1945. Al Meserlin, the last survivor present at the Nazi surrender proceedings in Rheims, France passed away in March of 2009.

UNCONDITIONAL SURRENDER
WITNESSING HISTORY – MAY 1945

"Unconditional surrender" – Nothing less was acceptable to the Allies fighting Nazi Germany during the Second World War in Europe then achieving this aim and goal. U.S. President Franklin D. Roosevelt first proclaimed this at a press conference in January 1943 following the Anglo-American summit meeting in Casablanca, French Morocco. After months of devastating war with Nazi Germany, he and British Prime Minister Winston Churchill vowed to never accept any armistice like that which led to the signing of the failed Versailles Peace Treaty after World War I. No, their mission was to win! Soviet Union Premier Joseph Stalin, who was not present at the summit, agreed in absentia. From that moment forward, the goal of absolute victory became the basis for every Allied military campaign and by mid-1945, victory was near.

Nazi Germany leader Adolf Hitler and his German Armed Forces High Command however, refused to surrender unconditionally to the Allies. Despite defeat after defeat on land, in the air and on the high seas, Hitler insisted on fighting. Resistance to unconditional surrender does end though upon Hitler committing suicide on April 30, 1945 and Grand Admiral Karl Donitz becoming his chosen successor.

CONCEDING DEFEAT

U nbeknownst to Hitler, just four days before his death, the first direct suggestion of surrender reached U.S. General Dwight D. Eisenhower, Commander of the Supreme Headquarters of the Allied Forces in Europe (SHAEF) in Rheims, France. It came in the form of a long message from Churchill to the General relaying a proposal from Heinrich Himmler, Nazi Germany's Minister of the Interior and head of the infamous Schutzstaffel (SS). Behind Hitler's back, Himmler offered to surrender the Western Front in Europe. Eisenhower reacted swiftly. No! No proposition, he said, should be entertained unless it involved the surrender of all German forces on all fronts to include those fighting the Soviets. Churchill and U.S. President Harry Truman, who succeeded President Roosevelt upon his passing on April 12, 1945, concurred. They so notified Soviet Premier Stalin. Meanwhile, Hitler upon learning of Himmler's proposal, dismissed the minister and had him arrested. However, days later, after Hitler's suicide, his chosen successor Admiral Donitz does reach out to the Allies to discuss surrender. As Germany's new leader, Donitz foresaw ultimate defeat and did not want to prolong the inevitable. In comparison, his terms were similar to Himmler's. Donitz orders his high command to initiate surrender talks only with the Americans and British. He and his leadership hoped that after surrendering to the Western Allies, the former enemies would then join with Nazi Germany to wage war against a common foe: the Soviet Union and counter its spread of Communism.

In the morning of May 5, a representative of Admiral Donitz arrived at Eisenhower's headquarters, formerly a schoolhouse for children, in Rheims, France. The General had received notice that he was coming the day before and passed this information onto the Soviet high command. In his message to the Russians, Eisenhower asked them to designate a Red Army officer to come to SHAEF headquarters as the Russian representative in the negotiations with Donitz's government. The Russian High Command thereafter designated Major General Ivan Suslaparov to be its representative. General Eisenhower designated his chief of staff Brigadier General Walter Bedell Smith to carry out the negotiations.

The German representative, General Admiral Hans von Friedeburg, asked initially to clear up a number of points. Without pause, General Smith informed Friedeburg there was no point discussing anything but unconditional and total surrender. The German admiral protested that he had no power to sign such a document. He requested permission to transmit a message to Donitz and shortly after doing so received a reply that Colonel General Alfred Jodl, Chief of Operations of the German High Command, was on his way to SHAEF headquarters to assist with the negotiations. Eisenhower now believed the Germans were playing for time so that they could withdraw military units from the Eastern Front and transfer them to the Western Front to avoid their capture by the Russians.

General Jodl arrives at SHAEF headquarters at 5:30 pm in the afternoon of May 5. In the evening, General Jodl met with General Smith and is told that unless the Germans ceased all delay, Eisenhower would close the entire Allied western front and by force prevent any German units from surrendering to the Western Allies. This stance provokes Jodl to immediately send a cable to Donitz requesting authority to agree to a complete surrender to become effective 48 hours after the signing. Eisenhower upon hearing this and not willing to tolerate any further delay informs Jodl through General Smith that the surrender must be signed immediately and become effective 48 hours from midnight, May 6. If not, the Western Front would be sealed at once. Being informed of this, Admiral Donitz sees the inevitability of compliance and authorizes Jodl to sign the surrender document.

SOLEMN SIGNING

The surrender takes place in the early morning hours of May 7 in the War Room at the Supreme Headquarters. The walls of the room are lined with battle maps charting Germany's defeat. General Jodl takes a seat before General Smith at the conference table in the room with his aide Major General Wilhelm Oxenius on his left and Grand Admiral von Friedeburg on his right. General Smith is flanked at the table by British Lieutenant General Frederick Morgan, SHAEF Deputy Chief of Staff; French Major General Francois Sevez, representative of General Alphonse Juin, French Chief of Staff and Soviet Major General Ivan Susloparov, the representative of the Soviet Chief of Staff. Jodl stoically signs the surrender document at 2:41 am on May 7 on behalf of Nazi Germany. All hostilities are to cease at midnight May 8, 1945. As observed by those witnessing the signing, there was a lack of emotion shown when the surrender document was signed. The German representatives sat militarily correct, all possessing stone like expressions. After the surrender document was signed by General Jodl, Brigadier General Walter Smith signs on behalf of the Allies with the French and Russian representatives signing thereafter as witnesses. Jodl then stands and gives a short speech in German asking that the German people be treated fairly. Not one of the Allied officers around the table displayed any elation at this ending of the long years of bitter fighting. What was experienced was a moment of solemn gratitude.

Eisenhower did not want to be present at the actual surrender, so after the surrender document was signed, General Jodl was then brought into Eisenhower's office. The Allied Supreme Commander immediately asked through an interpreter if Jodl thoroughly understood all the provisions of the document he had signed. "Ja" was the singular reply. Eisenhower then stated "You will officially and personally be held responsible if the terms of this surrender are violated, including its provisions for a German commander to appear in Berlin at the moment set by the Russian High Command to accomplish a formal surrender to that government. This is all." General Jodl then saluted and left the office.

After Jodl left, General Eisenhower and his staff then did celebrate the momentous occasion. Eisenhower with SHAEF Deputy Commander British Air Marshal Arthur Tedder on his left and General Smith on his right held up the two pens used in the actual signing and beamed a broad smile. Eisenhower after permitting photographers the opportunity to take pictures then went to the War Room to make a victory speech.

MISSION ACCOMPLISHED

Standing in the War Room in the old schoolhouse, Eisenhower makes a victory speech that was broadcast to all in the Allied nations. After making the speech, he then sends the Combined Chiefs of Staff the following message. "The mission of the Allied force was fulfilled at 0241, local time, May 7th, 1945."

Two days later, on May 9, the heads of the German armed services appear in Berlin to sign a ratification of the unconditional surrender document before the Soviet high command.

CHRONICLING HISTORY - EISENHOWER'S WARTIME PHOTOGRAPHER

Technical Sergeant Al Meserlin assigned to the U.S. Army's 3908th Signal Photo Battalion served as Supreme Commander General Eisenhower's personal wartime photographer. Appointed to the position on August 25, 1944, he met Eisenhower for the first time a few weeks later. From then on, Meserlin captured the Supreme Commander in moments both quiet and boisterous: conferring with Allied leaders, deliberating with his generals, directing the defeat of Nazi Germany, accepting the surrender of the armed forces of the Third Reich. Meserlin's photos are those most associated with the final phases of World War II, especially the famous pictures from May 7, 1945 of General Alfred Jodl unconditionally surrendering to the Allies on behalf of the German High Command. Meserlin recorded for posterity the actual signing of the surrender and General Eisenhower's victory speech from the War Room in the Rheims schoolhouse turned SHAEF Headquarters. His picture of Eisenhower's beaming "victory smile" captured the mood of that momentous morning.

After "Victory in Europe" was officially declared May 8, 1945, Meserlin wrote in his diary, "Never in my whole life of Army career have I ever thought I would be in the room when peace terms were taking place. How I ever received such a lucky break I'll never know."

In 2008, Al Meserlin donated his personal copies of all the

photos he took during the war to Brookdale Community College's Center for World War II Studies and Conflict Resolution, a Center which I founded and directed while a history professor at the College. He did so with the expressed desire that I display them via any means to enable all to better understand World War II and its impact. The Center thereafter established the Al Meserlin World War II Photo Gallery in a spacious lobby outside the college's Bankier Library. Meserlin died on March 22, 2009, the last survivor present at the Nazi surrender proceedings in Rheims, France.

What follows are the famous photos Meserlin took to officially record the unconditional surrender of Nazi Germany to the Allies in May 1945. They are being published in further fulfillment of Meserlin's expressed desire.

SUPREME HEADQUARTERS ALLIED EXPEDITIONARY FORCE PATCH

UNCONDITIONAL SURRENDER

U nconditional Surrender was the determined goal of the Allies fighting Nazi Germany during World War II in Europe. The goal was first announced by U.S. President Franklin D. Roosevelt at the Anglo-American summit held in Casablanca, French Morocco, in January 1943. Sitting with the President at the conference are French General Henri Giraud to his left, French General Charles De Gaulle to his immediate right and British Prime Minister Winston Churchill.

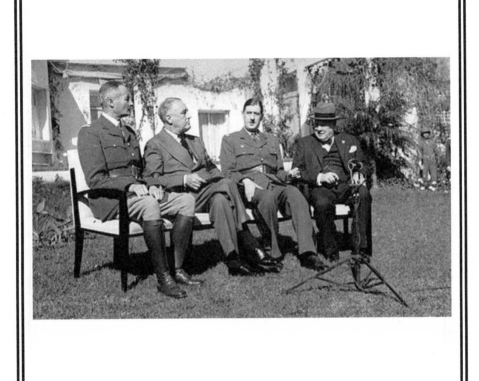

Unconditional Surrender Witnessing History – May 1945

HITLER'S SUCCESSOR

A dolf Hitler, wartime leader of Nazi Germany, committed suicide on April 30, 1945. Prior to his death, Hitler chose Grand Admiral Karl Donitz, Commander in Chief of the German Navy, to succeed him. Upon assuming the leadership of Nazi Germany, Donitz foresaw Germany's ultimate defeat and ordered his high command to initiate surrender talks with the Allies.

Paul E. Zigo

Unconditional Surrender Witnessing History – May 1945

GENERAL EISENHOWER URGES UNCONDITIONAL SURRENDER

U pon hearing from Prime Minister Winston Churchill that the Germans were proposing to surrender the Western Front to the Allies, U.S. General Dwight D. Eisenhower, Supreme Commander Allied Expeditionary Forces in Europe, maintained that no proposition be accepted or entertained unless it involved the surrender of *all* German forces on *all* war fronts, including those fighting the Russians' on the Eastern Front. The only way Nazi Germany could surrender per Eisenhower was unconditionally.

Unconditional Surrender Witnessing History – May 1945

ALLIED HEADQUARTERS, RHEIMS, FRANCE

Supreme Headquarters Allied Expeditionary Force (SHAEF) was established in a school house in Rheims, France after General Eisenhower chose to relocate his headquarters from Versailles to be closer to the front line and the fighting. Eisenhower moved his staff in February 1945, three months before Nazi Germany's unconditional surrender.

Unconditional Surrender Witnessing History – May 1945

GERMAN NEGOTIATOR

Grand Admiral Hans von Friedeburg arrives at SHAEF Headquarters the morning of May 5 to represent Grand Admiral Donitz and negotiate the surrender of Nazi Germany.

Paul E. Zigo

Unconditional Surrender Witnessing History – May 1945

EISENHOWER'S REPRESENTATIVE

After choosing not to be involved in negotiating the surrender terms, General Eisenhower designated his chief of staff, U.S. Lieutenant General Walter Bedell Smith to be his representative. General Smith meets with Germany's Admiral Friedeburg for the first time late in the morning of May 5.

Paul E. Zigo

Unconditional Surrender Witnessing History – May 1945

ARRIVING TO SURRENDER

Colonel General Alfred Jodl, Chief of Operations, German High Command, arrives at Rheims Airport via a US C-47 transport plane at 5:30 pm, May 5. General Jodl has been authorized by his government to complete a surrender agreement. A meeting with General Smith takes place soon after his arrival.

Unconditional Surrender Witnessing History – May 1945

ENROUTE TO SHAEF

General Jodl is being driven to SHAEF Headquarters to meet with U.S. General Walter Bedell Smith.

Paul E. Zigo

Unconditional Surrender Witnessing History – May 1945

ON THE VERGE OF SURRENDER

After meeting with General Smith regarding surrender terms, Colonel General Jodl cables Admiral Donitz in Berlin requesting permission for complete surrender to the Allies. He is authorized by Donitz to sign an unconditional surrender document to take effect shortly after midnight, May 8, 1945.

Paul E. Zigo

Unconditional Surrender Witnessing History – May 1945

ALL PARTIES PREPARE

I n the early hours of May 7, 1945, the German delegation take their seats in the War Room of SHAEF Headquarters, its walls lined with maps charting Nazi Germany's defeat.

Unconditional Surrender Witnessing History – May 1945

GERMAN DELEGATION

Seated at the War Room conference table across from U.S. General Walter Bedell Smith are German General Alfred Jodl, center, with his aide Major General Wilhelm Oxenius, left, and German Grand Admiral von Friedeberg, right.

Unconditional Surrender Witnessing History – May 1945

Allied Delegation

Eisenhower's Chief of Staff, U.S. Lieutenant General Walter Bedell Smith, center, presenting the unconditional surrender terms to the German delegation. Smith is flanked by, seated left to right, British Lieutenant General Frederick Morgan, SHAEF Deputy Chief of Staff; French Major General Francois Sevez, representative of General Alphonse Juin, French Chief of Staff; British Admiral Sir Harold M. Burrough, Commander, Allied Naval Expeditionary Forces; and Soviet Major General Ivan Susloparov, representative of the Soviet Chief of Staff.

Unconditional Surrender Witnessing History – May 1945

REVIEWING SURRENDER TERMS

Having acknowledged that Germany will surrender, General Jodl reviews the surrender documents. Standing behind him is British Major General Harold R. Bull, SHAEF G3 (Operations), who served as interpreter.

Unconditional Surrender Witnessing History – May 1945

PRIOR TO SIGNING
SURRENDER TERMS

German Colonel General Jodl, Chief of Staff, German Army, standing, is asked if the Germans understand the unconditional surrender terms and if he is prepared to sign the document. General Jodl answers "Ja."

Unconditional Surrender Witnessing History – May 1945

SIGNING SURRENDER DOCUMENT

At 0241 hours the morning of May 7, German Colonel General Alfred Jodl, Chief of Operations, German High Command, signs the document surrendering Nazi Germany unconditionally to the Allies as his aide, Major Wilhelm Oxenius, looks on. All hostilities are to cease by midnight May 8. U.S. General Smith then signs the document on behalf of the Allies.

Paul E. Zigo

Unconditional Surrender Witnessing History – May 1945

SOVIETS SIGN SURRENDER DOCUMENT

M ajor General Ivan Susloparov, representative of the Soviet Chief of Staff, signs the surrender document as U.S. General Carl Spaatz, Commander of US Army Air Forces in Europe, witnesses. French General Francois Sevel representing France signs afterwards.

Unconditional Surrender Witnessing History – May 1945

UNCONDITIONAL SURRENDER

The fully-signed surrender document executed at SHAEF Headquarters on the 7th day of May 1945 at 0241 hours.

Paul E. Zigo

ACT OF MILITARY SURRENDER - GERMAN

1. We the undersigned, acting by authority of the German High Command, hereby surrender unconditionally to the Supreme Commander, Allied Expeditionary Force and simultaneously to the Soviet High Command all forces on land, sea, and in the air who are at this date under German control.

2. The German High Command will at once issue orders to all German military, naval and air authorities and to all forces under German control to cease active operations at 2301 hours Central European time on 8 May and to remain in the positions occupied at that time. No ship, vessel, or aircraft is to be scuttled, or any damage done to their hull, machinery or equipment.

3. The German High Command will at once issue to the appropriate commanders, and ensure the carrying out of any further orders issued by the Supreme Commander, Allied Expeditionary Force and by the Soviet High Command.

4. This act of military surrender is without prejudice to, and will be superseded by any general instrument of surrender imposed by, or on behalf of the United Nations and applicable to GERMANY and the German armed forces as a whole.

5. In the event of the German High Command or any of the forces under their control failing to act in accordance with this Act of Surrender, the Supreme Commander, Allied Expeditionary Force and the Soviet High Command will take such punitive or other action as they deem appropriate.

Signed at *Rheims at 0241* on the 7th day of May, 1945.
France

On behalf of the German High Command.

[signature]

IN THE PRESENCE OF

On behalf of the Supreme Commander,
Allied Expeditionary Force,

On behalf of the Soviet
High Command,

[signatures]

- 2 -

AFTER THE SIGNING

The German delegation prepares to leave the War Room following their unconditional surrender. In the right rear, General Dwight D. Eisenhower's personal wartime photographer, Tech Sergeant Al Meserlin, is seen standing on an elevated platform holding his camera.

Paul E. Zigo

Unconditional Surrender Witnessing History – May 1945

Somber Departure

After the surrender document was signed, German General Jodl leaves the War Room and is brought to General Eisenhower's office.

Unconditional Surrender Witnessing History – May 1945

Awaiting General Jodl's Appearance

General Eisenhower, Supreme Allied Commander, who did not want to be present at the signing of the surrender document, waits for General Jodl to appear in his office. Upon arriving, Jodl is asked by Eisenhower through an interpreter if he thoroughly understands the provisions of the document he had signed. Jodl says "Ja" and then leaves the office.

Paul E. Zigo

Unconditional Surrender Witnessing History – May 1945

EISENHOWER SHOWING
SURRENDER PENS

After General Jodl leaves Eisenhower's office, U.S. Navy Captain Harry Butcher, naval aide to General Eisenhower, hands him the pens used to sign the surrender document. Joining in enjoying the moment, pictured left to right, are Soviet General Ivan Susloparov, USSR representative; British Lieutenant General Sir Frederick Morgan, SHAEF Deputy Chief of Staff; U.S. Lieutenant General Walter Bedell Smith, SHAEF Chief of Staff; U.S. Navy Captain Harry Butcher; and British Air Chief Marshal Sir Arthur Tedder, Deputy Commander, SHAEF.

Unconditional Surrender Witnessing History – May 1945

VICTORY SMILE

Permitting photographers to take pictures of the momentous moments in his office, General Eisenhower is captured beaming this unforgettable "victory smile." He then sends the Combined Chiefs of Staff a simple message, "The mission of this Allied force was fulfilled at 0241 local time, May 7, 1945."

Unconditional Surrender Witnessing History – May 1945

GENERAL EISENHOWER ANNOUNCES VICTORY

General Eisenhower, Supreme Allied Commander, with SHAEF Deputy Commander, British Air Chief Sir Arthur Tedder beside him, makes a "victory speech" that was broadcast throughout Europe from the SHAEF Headquarters War Room. Eisenhower, speaking briefly without any prepared notes, announces the end of the war in Europe.

Unconditional Surrender Witnessing History – May 1945

VICTORY PARADE IN RHEIMS, FRANCE, MAY 1945

Right after Victory in Europe (VE) Day was announced, the city of Rheims celebrated the Allied triumph with a victory parade. Citizens stand everywhere, even on the tops of the tallest buildings in the city, to watch the parade. Pictured is a float carrying Adolf Hitler in effigy.

Paul E. Zigo

Unconditional Surrender Witnessing History – May 1945

VIVE LA FRANCE!

French children wave their country's flag during the May 1945 Victory Parade in Rheims, celebrating a future free of Nazi domination.

Paul E. Zigo

Unconditional Surrender Witnessing History – May 1945

FRENCH CHILD AT THE RHEIMS VICTORY PARADE

In this endearing photo, a young French female child is seen waving an American flag during the Rheims Victory parade. This is one of Tech Sergeant Al Meserlin's last photos taken in Europe

Unconditional Surrender Witnessing History – May 1945

TECH SERGEANT (T5) AL MESERLIN

Tech Sergeant Al Meserlin, assigned to the U.S. Army's 3908 Signal Photo Battalion, was chosen to be General Dwight D. Eisenhower's personal wartime photographer in August 1944. He met with General Eisenhower for the first time the next month and from then on photographed the general conferring with Allied leaders, conferencing with his commanders, visiting his troops, and accepting the unconditional surrender of the armed forces of Nazi Germany on May 7, 1945. Meserlin's photos are those most associated with the final phase of the war in Europe.

Unconditional Surrender Witnessing History – May 1945

ABOUT THE AUTHOR

PAUL E. ZIGO, a history professor, author and military historian is the founder and director, of the World War II Era Studies Institute. The institute is dedicated to furthering one's knowledge and understanding of the WW II era and its impact on history. He is a graduate of Temple University and the United States Army War College. He authored and edited in 2009 *Witnessing History: The Eisenhower Photographs* featuring all the photos of General Dwight D. Eisenhower taken by his personal wartime photographer, Al Meserlin. Zigo was also the executive producer and narrator of the cable network series *Triumphant Spirit: America's World War II Generation Speaks* from 2001 to 2004. In 2014, he authored the book *The Longest Walk: The Amazing Story of the 29th Inf. Division on D-Day 6 June 1944* and in 2017, he co-authored the book *Bataan – When Men Have To Die*, an accounting of the fall of the Philippine Islands to the Japanese in 1942. Mr. Zigo is a 30 year veteran of the United States Army retiring as a Colonel and is a founding member of the National Museum of the US Army.